That's Not Canadian:

A SEARCH FOR HUMAN RIGHTS IN A GLOBAL PANDEMIC

By: Dr. Sharon Ryan

Gotham Books

30 N Gould St.
Ste. 20820, Sheridan, WY 82801
https://gothambooksinc.com/

Phone: 1 (307) 464-7800

© 2024 *Dr. Sharon Ryan*. All rights reserved.

No part of this book may be reproduced, stored in a retrieval system, or transmitted by any means without the written permission of the author.

Published by Gotham Books (July 24, 2024)

ISBN: 979-8-3303-4133-7 (H)
ISBN: 979-8-3303-4381-2 (P)
ISBN: 979-8-3303-4382-9 (E)

Because of the dynamic nature of the Internet, any web addresses or links contained in this book may have changed since publication and may no longer be valid.

The views expressed in this work are solely those of the author and do not necessarily reflect the views of the publisher, and the publisher hereby disclaims any responsibility for them.

Credit for front picture given to Edmonton Journal, Greg Southam.

"Material republished with the express permission of: Edmonton Journal, a division of Postmedia Network Inc."

TABLE OF CONTENTS

INTRODUCTION
    This is No Fairy Tale vii

Prologue
    Chaos in Continuing Care Facilities, Unlawful Orders, and Heartless Leadership x

Chapter 1
    A Very Canadian Life 3

Chapter 2
    A Very Canadian Doctor 6

Chapter 3
    A Very Early Morning 12

Chapter 4
    A Very Awkward Christmas 17

Chapter 5
    A Very Awkward New Year's Eve 18

Chapter 6
    A Very Bad Cough 22

Chapter 7
    Heaven Speaks 26

Chapter 8
    Life is Fun in Palliative Care! 31

Chapter 9
Paradise Continued...**39**

Chapter 10
Paradise Lost: Locked Out!...**46**

Chapter 11
The Sound of Silence..**50**

Chapter 12
Calling in the Big Guns..**56**

Chapter 13
A Very Canadian MLA and a Premier with Wisdom......**69**

Chapter 14
Paradise Restored: "I'm In!"..**74**

Chapter 15
A Passing into a New Life..**83**

INTRODUCTION

This is No Fairy Tale

Once upon a time, in a land far, far away, there lived a really nice bunch of people known as CAN-EH-D-ANNS. They were a really, really polite bunch of people. They always worked hard without complaining and always paid their taxes.

CAN-EH-D-ANNS had a quirky way of talking that the rest of the world found a little bit funny. They would often end their sentences with the word "Eh" and hence they became known as CAN-EH-D-ANNS.

They were known for being very nice and always got along with each other no matter where in the world their fellow citizens came from. People from all over the world moved to CAN-EH-DA! They came from India, China, Philippines, Europe, South America, Jamaica, Eastern Europe, Africa, etc. because they all knew that the people of CAN-EH-DA! were friendly. And that's why the sound "DA!" finishes the name of the county. It's like they would say to each other, "Life is really hard here. Where should we move to?" And everyone would say, "Well, we heard that CAN-EH-DA! is really friendly so …. "DA!" …. Let's move there!

And so it went year after year in CAN-EH-DA! The people worked hard and helped each other out as much as possible. One special characteristic of CAN-EH-D-ANNS was that they always showed a special appreciation for vulnerable people – like the sick and elderly. They built wonderful facilities to help these vulnerable people. And the younger people from every country would work in these marvelous facilities to ensure that the sick and elderly had the very best care.

In fact, CAN-EH-DA! gained a reputation around the world as being a compassionate and caring country. It was a peaceful and prosperous place to live. And they only thing anyone every complained about was the cold, cold winters.

The winters were so cold in CAN-EH-DA! that every bug that ever inhabited your garden or home would be instantly killed when winter set in. So it was a pretty good system if you think about it.

Everything was moving along just peachy in CAN-EH-DA! when suddenly a tiny but dangerous virus called COVID-19 decided to move to the country because it heard that the people were so polite, they wouldn't mind if it lived there. So COVID-19 moved in and suddenly a terrible spell was cast upon the people and they became very sleepy. Some of the leaders of CAN-EH-DA! became quite unkind and ordered that the residents of CAN-EH-DA forget about the sick and elderly. They forgot that CAN-EH-D-ANNS really loved the sick and elderly people and cared for them A LOT.

These sleepy leaders had the power to lock CAN-EH-DA! sick and elderly people inside the beautiful facilities the people had built for them with their taxes and wouldn't even let the people inside to visit them! It was really, really horrible.

Very soon, the sick and elderly people found themselves isolated and alone and many of them had to die alone without their beautiful families surrounding them. The beautiful facilities turned into ugly prisons and many seniors went without water and food and even had to live in excrement because the beautiful people of the world that came to help CAN-EH-DA! weren't allowed inside all of the facilities to help them.

It was a very sad time for all.

Then one day a few CAN-EH-D-ANNs woke up from their deep slumber and they knew that the leaders had been placed under a terrible spell of cruelty. So they tried to wake them up and they yelled really, really loudly, "Hey leaders! Did you forget that we love our sick and elderly? How about letting us inside to help them, eh?"

Finally, the leaders woke up and let the people of CAN-EH-DA! inside to visit and help the sick and elderly and eventually they even managed to kick COVID out of the nice country. DA!

The moral of the story is when you are faced with a difficult challenge, don't forget who you are. Use your wild imagination to navigate through the problem while keeping your values intact.

Because solving problems with a mean spirit and cruel ideas – well, that's just NOT CANADIAN. Eh?

Prologue

Chaos in Continuing Care Facilities, Unlawful Orders, and Heartless Leadership

My mother was in the first wave of seniors to be locked inside a palliative care ward in the first wave of the pandemic in March 2020.

I was thrown into a situation I could never have imagined in a desperate fight to win back our visitation rights so my mother would not have to die alone.

This is our story.

Chaos in Continuing Care Facilities

Seniors across Canada were forced to live and die alone as a result of heartless and thoughtless decision making by our medical and political leaders. And just so the reader doesn't think I am too sensitive to the issue, I thought a good place to start is at the end with an independent report summarizing what had happened at continuing care facilities. This is not fiction.

In February, 2023, the Auditor General of Alberta released a report that analyzed the public health response by Alberta

Health and Alberta Health Services to COVID-19 in 355 publicly funded continuing care facilities in Alberta. The study covers the period of time from March to December 2020 when 379 outbreaks occurred in continuing care facilities and resulting in 1000 deaths in Alberta.

The report covers what the authors call "crucial activities" for success: planning, communicating, executing, and monitoring and enforcing compliance. The findings include realizations such as:

1. Planning exercises lacked emergency preparedness among key participants such as Alberta Health, AHS and facility operators.
2. Orders of the Chief Medical Officer of Health caused confusion and frustration at the facilities,
3. Lack of adequate staff to provide resident care
4. Residents faced dangerous levels of dehydration, insufficient meals, inadequate pain management, poor hygiene, and dirty rooms.
5. Facilities had dangerously high temperatures and poor air quality.

Although the report proclaims that "communicating" is one of the four crucial activities, it never acknowledged the shameless and sloppy way in which family members were notified (and NOT notified) of COVID-19 CMOH ORDERS restricting visitors and leaving the residents in emotionally painful isolation.

In my particular case, I was NOT notified of the very first lock-out order until I arrived at the facility front door to find it locked. I collapsed on the bench in the parking lot in shock at the realization that I could no longer see my mother as she lay in that palliative care facility dying alone and in confusion as to why she had been abandoned by her family.

I thought that our story going on the front page of the Edmonton Journal and on CTV National News along with other families' stories would alert the health care leaders to this glaring lapse in ethical judgement but alas it didn't. Three years later with the release of this long-awaited report, communication of Orders to family members has not been addressed in any meaningful way.

Orders of Alberta's Chief Medical Officer were Unlawful

Throughout Canada, Chief Medical Officers in each province issued orders ranging from locking out visitors from palliative care wards, isolating residents of continuing care facilities, closing schools, mandating mask wearing and social distancing, shutting down businesses, denying unvaccinated persons employment, etc.

These sudden and prolonged measures forced small business owners into bankruptcy, devasted families, denied students in class education, robbed children of their birthday parties, triggered suicides, fueled depression and anxiety disorders, thwarted Canadian's religious rights and freedoms, and isolated seniors and dying people from access to their loved ones in the final months and years of their lives.

These measures stripped Canadians from their constitutional rights to enjoy their lives with the freedom and democracy that make-up the very fabric of this country. We were unrecognizable as a nation.

Now three years later, courts have ruled that the orders issued were unlawful and void. Justice Romain, in a 90-page decision agreed that the orders were issued by cabinet rather than the Chief Medical Officer and so they were politically influenced.

Furthermore, even if the Chief Medical Officer had issued these orders without cabinet influence, her power was never intended to last for several years but only as a temporary measure in the midst of a health crisis.

Constitutional lawyers are now speaking up about the dangers of the centralization of power in the hands of one person, which has a tendency to result in tyranny, especially when that person is not democratically accountable.

These lawyers warn that legislative reform is necessary to hold these decision makers accountable and that deliberation by a wide range of experts needs to be part of the plan when these decisions affect every aspect of Canadians' lives from health to economic aspects.

All I know is that the whole thing seemed absurd to me as I was caught directly in the path of this tyranny. In one day, our entire country was unrecognizable and few people stood up to protest because of course protesting rights were stripped from us too.

If we ever face such absurdity again, let's remember what it means to be Canadian and stop government leaders from stripping us of the core values this country represents.

My Take on It All

The leaders during Covid made sweeping decisions without seemingly giving careful consideration to the infringement they had on limiting fundamental rights and freedoms of Canadian citizens. In doing so, they crossed a few lines that represent what it means to be Canadian.

Fundamental Freedoms. The *Canadian Charter of Rights and Freedoms* defines Canadians' fundamental freedoms such as freedom of conscience and religion, thought, belief, opinion and expression.

Canadian citizens freedom of religion was thwarted by the sudden lockdown measures the government imposed upon our seniors and dying Canadians. Palliative care wards and seniors' housing facilities were locked up suddenly preventing loved ones from saying goodbye and being present while their mothers, fathers, and grandparents died alone.

These actions prevented these dying people their fundamental right to access their religious practices surrounding death such as having a loved one provide them comfort with prayers by their bedside, restricting priests and ministers from anointing the sick and dying, receiving the sacrament of penance and reconciliation considered necessary by some faiths in ensuring the person enters heaven in the afterlife.

I am aware that the Canadian Charter of Rights and Freedoms does contain a statutory provision that limits the freedoms of Canadians if the government of Canada deems that such limits are justifiable and reasonable – such as a pandemic that affects the health and lives of nearly everyone.

I lost faith in our government's ability to consider the enormity of human suffering they imposed on Canadians by instituting blanket lock-out orders on palliative care and seniors' housing facilities without considering gross violation upon the religious right and freedoms of these people.

I underestimated the shockingly callous and swift orders instituted by our chief medical officers in isolating our palliative care and seniors housing facility residents allowing them to die alone and, in some instances, to fester without water, food, and basic medical care.

As my own mother was one of these palliative care patients caught in the first wave of the pandemic, I was on the front line of it all and witnessed first-hand the torturous conditions the patients, nurses, and doctors faced when a few government officials pulled the rug right out from under them and all of us.

THAT'S NOT CANADIAN. It's NOT Canadian to isolate our seniors and dying relatives and let them suffer in silence and confusion while facing death.

It's NOT Canadian to take away any person's religious freedoms.

It's NOT Canadian to take a leadership role in this country and then demonstrate to the rest of us that you have limited moral imagination to understand the suffering your decisions impose of the very citizens that built this country.

It was those seniors who worked their whole lives, raised families, paid the taxes that built the medical schools these leaders attended only to have these very people turn their backs on them in their hour of need. THAT'S NOT Canadian.

It's NOT Canadian to lack compassion and watch vulnerable people suffer, tying the hands of their family members, and hide under poorly written clauses in legislation.

Canadians are compassionate and caring. Canadians are appreciative when they advance in society on the backs of those who labored to build the institutions that gave the privileged professionals their careers and quality of life.

Canadians love their religious expression and Canadians are trustworthy and kind.

Canadians have a set of values that define this county including but not limited to: respect for everyone, love your neighbor, help those in need, look out for the vulnerable, feed the hungry, cloth the single parent and his and her children, care for the elderly, put money in the Red Kettle every Christmas when shopping at Costco, and never ever park in a designated handicapped parking stall!

That's what it means to be Canadian.

I hope this story sheds a bit of light on how much Canadians treasure the tender hearts of our seniors and dying loved ones so that the moral imagination of the reader is stretched – especially if that reader is a political or medial leader because ignoring the pleas of our vulnerable citizens – well, that's just NOT Canadian.

That's Not Canadian:

A SEARCH FOR HUMAN RIGHTS IN A GLOBAL PANDEMIC

Chapter 1

A Very Canadian Life

December 2019

It was another gloomy Friday in wintery Edmonton as I made my way through traffic to pick up my mom, Louise, for her weekly bridge game at the St. Albert Senior's Centre.

As usual, my heartbeat was racing in my effort to get her in time for the 1:00 p.m. start time – no exceptions!

The hardest part for me were carving out three hours of every Friday afternoon for her favorite outing of the week. Louise always prepared herself meticulously for the games. She dressed sharply and always had her nails creatively done.

I pulled up sharply at noon and stormed my way into her house with my regular loud announcement of my arrival, "Hey Mom. Are you ready? Let's go so we have time for an egg salad sandwich and coffee before the game!"

Louise was always calm and cheerful. No matter how flustered I would become, my mom would never buy into that game, which is probably why she managed to live so long. She was ninety and in perfect health!

"Coming, Sharon. Just need to find my purse." Then she appeared out of her bedroom, looking radiant and ready for an afternoon out on the town.

Slowing and deliberately, she put on her coat in her usual manner and struggled with her buttons. "There. Let's go!"

The two of us piled our way out of her house and into my car. On the way, we would always get caught up on each other's week and plan our bridge playing strategy.

"Let's go over how we bid if either of us gets 21 points."

"Mom," I would retort, "we never get 21 points. How about if we simply review how we bid if either one of us gets 6 to 8 points?"

As if she never heard me, Louise would always proceed to read out the bidding protocol for 21 points. This is how Louise and I learned how to play bridge. No wonder we rarely won!

But we always had a great time. No matter the outcome, every situation my mom ever encountered was always, always fun and positive. It was just her natural way of being in the world.

No matter how positive she was, nothing could have prepared us for what was to come. A global pandemic that rushed into our lives and tested our deepest resolve and values at the very core.

So, there we were at the bridge table once again. Bidding commenced. As usual I got average cards and as usual, Louise sent me signals that she had an awesome hand with 21 points.

As if on cue, I bite the bait and raised our bidding in response to her very large opening bid. Over bid and underplayed. That was our pattern. Nothing new today.

Then suddenly something new started to happened. Something I had never experienced before. Joyful Louise suddenly started to look pretty grey. Her hands went limp and she wiggled uncomfortably in her chair.

"Hurry up and bid," one woman snipped at her.

"Sharon. I am not well. Let's go home." Three words I have never hear Louise ever say – ever. Go home? Louise never missed an opportunity to play another hour, shop another hour, party another hour. But her time was up and she knew it.

"Can't you at least finish the hand?" the woman yelled.

I got up from my chair and went over to my mother's side and helped her stand up. She leaned all her weight into me as we waddled out of the room – tears filling my eyes. Somehow, I knew this would be her last bridge game.

A good bridge game on a Friday afternoon with coffee and egg salad sandwiches is Canadian – it's VERY CANADIAN.

Chapter 2

A Very Canadian Doctor

December 2019

I piled Louise into my car and we headed home. Very soon thereafter she said to me, "Something's wrong inside. I just don't feel right."

Decision time. Do we let her sleep it off, go to the nearest walk-in clinic, or head to emergency?

Sleeping it off didn't seem like a very good idea to me. In her whole life, my mother never said anything like, "something's wrong inside." Louise was 90 years old and in very good health. She was active, taking care of her own household and could shop like nobody's business.

"Shop 'til we drop," we used to say to each other.

Going to the nearest medical clinic didn't seem like such a good idea either. As anyone could tell you, a patient could wait three hours or longer to see a doctor. Since she had an internal pain, it would be uncomfortable for her to sit that long in a waiting room.

It's at times like these I wish family doctors would make house calls. In the old days, the local doctor would hitch up his horse and head on over to see what's wrong with his 90-year-old patient. Today that is unheard of.

My father attended the same clinic for over 40 years! In the final weeks of his life, we couldn't bribe a physician to drop by and renew his prescription. Rather we had to pick up this six-foot-two inches tall frame of man, place him in a wheelchair, roll him out to the parking lot and somehow lift him out of the wheelchair into the car. Then when we arrived at the medical clinic, same routine – different building. There he would sit for an hour or longer in a crowded waiting room full of sick people only to shuffle his way into an examination room for 10 minutes with a doctor. Wow!

So that left me with one option – head to the nearest emergency room. And so I packed Louise's purse full of snacks and away we went to the Sturgeon Hospital in St. Albert.

Upon arriving, I drove my car right up to the door in order to find a wheelchair and haul her in. Within minutes, she saw the triage nurse who then told us to wait in the waiting room. Mere minutes after that, we were in an examination room. Amen to triage nurses!

Louise lay on the examination table comfortably – shoes off, covered in a blanket. I encouraged her to have a little nap. Eventually the emergency doctor walked in. He was a friendly compassionate doctor with excellent conversation skills. He had us smiling within just a few minutes.

After examining Louise, the doctor ordered an X-Ray. Several hours later the X-Ray was done and the results were in his hands He explained that he noticed something in the image, consulted with an internal medicine specialist, and they both agreed that a CAT scan was necessary in order for them to determine the exact cause of Louise's internal pain.

Several hours later the CAT scan was in the doctor's hands.

By this time, it was 1:00 a.m. We were all exhausted – me, my mom, and the doctor. Nevertheless, he remained friendly and patient.

"Louise," he started, "I don't have good news." Both Mom and I took a deep breath and remained deeply silent listening for the very next word.

"I have consulted with a cancer specialist and it appears that you have some cancer cells in the pancreas. Now this type of cancer is quite aggressive and what concerns us is that it appears it have spread to the stomach. Louise, I need to be completely honest with you . . . typically, this type of cancer spreads very quickly. We need to talk about treatment options."

I remember the seconds following the doctor's last sentence. Both Mom and I remained absolutely still and silent. Complete shock is what I was feeling buuuuttt apparently Louise was not so surprised, although I was completely surprised by her reaction:

"Oh well. I've lived a good life. Let's go home!" as she proceeded to jump off the examination table.

Shock. I was in complete shock with both the diagnosis and my mother's reaction to it. And then shock again with what followed!

As Louise proceeded to jump off the examination table, the doctor stopped her abrupt fall to the floor. He reached out his arm to catch her in midair and gently placed her back on the examination table. Disaster averted!

"Not so fast, Louise!" he exclaimed. "I think it's best if we take a bit of time and talk about treatment options. Would you like to see the CAT scan?"

"Yes," said both Louise and I in synchronicity.

The doctor proceeded to help Louise off the examination table. I took her by the arm and the three of us walked across the emergency room floor to the machine that shows the results.

To be honest, all I saw was a bunch of grey matter, but the doctor proceeded to show the even denser grey matter surrounding Mom's pancreas and stomach.

"See," he said, "this area here is your pancreas. Here is the stomach. This grey matter here is the cancer that is growing in those areas."

The three of us proceeded to walk slowly back to the examination room to talk about next steps.

Well, knowing Louise's zest for life and action, I pretty much knew how this next part of the conversation would go.

"I have spoken with a cancer specialist just a few moments ago and we have reviewed some next steps," the doctor said.

Oh man, I was thinking to myself. Here we go with a torturous cancer regime that would not only kill Louise, but her spirit too. Oh well, let's hear it.

The doctor continued, "We can book you in for a visit at the Cross Cancer Institute and determine which regime would be best for you."

'Oh God, help us!" I said inside. "We all know how that will go."

"But," the doctor continued, "to be perfectly honest with you, Louise, the prognosis is quite uncertain. Pancreatic cancer is very aggressive and although we can try our best to curtail it . . .."

Say no more doctor. I think we are all on the same page.

"No!" Exclaimed Louise with absolute confidence, "I will not undergo cancer treatment. I am happy with my life and I am happy to move on. I don't want to prolong this agony unnecessarily. Let's go home, Sharon."

On that note, we thanked the doctor for his time and compassionate care and slowly exited the hospital to the car.

The drive home seemed slow. What am I supposed to do now? How do you be with someone you love upon learning that they will die soon – very soon?

I drove Mom home. Escorted her slowly out of the car and into her house. I helped her get ready for bed and told her I would stay the night but that I had to get up early in the morning to administer a final exam at MacEwan University.

First, though, I had to drive to a 24-hour pharmacy and get her prescription filled. By the time I arrived back at her house, it was 3:00 a.m. I gave her the prescription and collapsed in the spare bedroom.

Compassionate doctors who work long into the wee hours of the night to comfort dying patients ... now THAT'S CANADIAN .... That's very Canadian. Thank you, E.R doctors!

Chapter 3

A Very Early Morning

December 2019

Six a.m. came quickly. Just three hours sleep with shocking news regarding the most important person in my life. My mother was feeling great one moment and then half-a-day later given a death sentence and three months left to live.

Life goes on. I had to administer a final exam at MacEwan University at 9:00 a.m. It was my first experience with "team teaching," which means a collaborative approach to the delivery of education.

I slept over at my mom's house for obvious reasons. When my alarm went off, I pulled myself out of bed, poured myself a cup of coffee, checked up on Mom and headed out the door.

In a dark and freezing December morning, I drove myself from St. Albert to MacEwan University in downtown Edmonton in a daze. Utterly exhausted, I arrived at 8:55 a.m. and headed directly to my office to hopefully find the final exams.

No. They were nowhere in sight. Did I miss a memo? I frantically searched my emails for intel on where the final exams were being held. Nothing came up.

So, I rambled down the hallway into the examination room where about four hundred students sat waiting for their exam. Luckily, another teacher on the "team" had arrived early and retrieved the final exams and began distributing them.

Seeing that everything was under control, I headed to the side of the auditorium and found a stair that I could sit on while the students wrote their exam. I had never been more exhausted in life! I could barely keep my eyes open through the two-hour ordeal.

I wanted to tell someone what I had just gone through but of course there was no one to talk to in the middle of a final exam. So, I just suffered in silence.

At the end of the exam, I dragged myself out of the room and headed to my car back to St. Albert – numb.

I went directly to Mom's home. She was still sleeping. I got on the phone and let all the siblings know about the doctor's prognosis. The next step was to take Mom into the Cross Cancer Institute for a biopsy so that we could know if the doctor's prognosis was correct.

Mom eventually woke up and we sat and had coffee and toast like any other morning. Only this morning was unlike any other morning we had ever had. How do you have small talk with someone you love who has just had it announced to her that she only had a few months left to live?

The next few hours were filled with some family members coming over and visiting. Left alone with Mom again, it was soon supper time and we did what we always love to do – order our meals from Skip the Dishes and watch some great TV shows.

Our food arrived and I poured Mom and me a large glass of red wine. We sat comfortably in front of the TV set and began surfing the channels to find something interesting to watch. Normally we feasted on the golden oldie movies from the fifties. Tonight, for some strange reason, we landed on a religious channel and watched a show I had never seen before - *Turning Point by American evangelical Christian author, David Jeremiah.*

This show featured his new book, *Revealing the Mysteries of Heaven*. How appropriate! Mom and I began chomping our lovely meal – Swiss Chalet roast chicken and baked potato with coleslaw – and sipping our wine.

It wasn't too far into the show when we both became extremely engaged with the content: What happens when we die? Where do we go? Is there an afterlife?

Dr. Jeremiah was an eloquent speaker with a soothing voice. Both Louise and I listened with intent interest as we enjoyed our wonderful meal and wine.

At the end of the program, an infomercial came on encouraging the viewers to call the 1-800 number to order a copy of Dr. Jeremiah's book. "Write that down, Sharon." Mom cried out. "Order that book. Order it!"

I didn't hesitate for two seconds. I picked up my phone and dialed the 1-800 number. A lovely call centre attendant answered the phone, "Turning Point. How can I help you?" I quickly put the phone on speaker phone so Mom could hear the conversation.

"Hi." I said, "I'd like to order *Revealing the Mysteries of Heaven* please."

"Oh," she said, "We are all sold out and there is a long back-order list. Would you like me to put you on back-order?"

"Well, how long is the back-order?" I asked.

"Hard to say. Perhaps three months or longer," she answered.

"Three months?" I yelled at the top of my voice. "We don't have three months. We need to figure out how to get into heaven NOW."

Both Louise and I laughed at the top of our lungs. We both found that pretty funny.

The call centre attendant was speechless.

"Um," she said, "well, I do have one copy on my desk. How about if I just mail that one to you?"

"Perfect," I said.

Done like dinner. Louise and I had enjoyed out Swiss Chalet chicken and red wine, a fabulous show by Dr. Jeremiah and a great laugh with a call centre attendant.

Now all we had to do was to figure out how to get through the rest of the night and we would be fine.

Eventually, I put Mom to bed and went upstairs to my temporary bedroom – exhausted beyond all words.

Swiss Chalet roast chicken with a baked potato and coleslaw delivered by a Skip-the-Dishes driver – now THAT'S CANADIAN!

Chapter 4

A Very Awkward Christmas

December 2019

I have no memory of that Christmas except the entire family travelled from everywhere to be together with Mom.

Children and grandchildren who travel across the country to be with Grandma and Grandpa, now THAT'S CANADIAN.

Chapter 5

A Very Awkward New Year's Eve

January 2020

Mom and I had always planned a fun New Year's Eve party. This year would be no different with one exception – we had to get our little trip to the hospital out of the way.

Because the emergency room doctors diagnosed Mom's cancer as advanced and aggressive in the pancreas with it heading directly to her stomach, they fast tracked her biopsy and so we were heading out on New Year's Eve to have Louise's biopsy. Happy New Year!!

We were given strict and specific instructions from everything from where to park to where to go for the procedure.

We entered a waiting room full of other exuberant people so excited to be getting medical procedures done on New Year's Eve! What a joyous crowd!

I immediately put out of mind the timing of our visit and focused on getting Louise to the right place at the right time. Within minutes we were escorted to a large holding area with about 10 beds, all with curtains around them.

The nurse came over to us and helped Mom change into a gown. My sister, Sandy, and I waited by her bedside. It was a few hours before it was her turn for the biopsy. In that time, I had noticed the wide array of other patients waiting in the que.

In particular, one young mother, very frail, was there with her husband by her side. From the phone calls they were getting, I had determined that they had two young girls at home. How sad. They both looked exhausted and resigned to their fate. Mom had very little time left on this earth and soon Dad would be both mom and dad to their very young children.

In fact, every patient in that room was near death. The nurses were so lovely, helpful, and cheerful to each one of them. They really and truly cared about every sick person in there.

I kept over-hearing the conversations in the room. One woman had a terribly violent cough. She was reflecting to her friends how she had just got home from Christmas in New York and landed with this cough in the lungs.

I wasn't too concerned about her being so close to us as we had bigger problems – like what will this biopsy show was happening to my mother.

After several hours of waiting, Louise and I were escorted to another waiting room closer to the doctor who would do the biopsy. In just a few minutes, his nurse took both Louise and I into the small examination room where the soft-spoken doctor introduced himself and explained the procedure.

I stood by Louise for the duration of the procedure and she was very calm – as always. The doctor remained quiet and reserved as he examined through the medical equipment the state of Mom's pancreas and stomach.

I sensed immediately that the news was not good. He had a very soft and compassionate look on his face and I knew – it wasn't good.

He told us they would send the results to Louise's family doctor and we should hear from him within the week.

After the biopsy, Mom, Sandy, and I headed back home. Sandy went back to her family for New Year's Eve and I stayed with Mom. We did what we always love to do on New Year's Eve – prepare a very nice meal, drink wine and champaign and watch old movies and live TV.

Mom was always the best companion I ever had – in all occasions. Even after spending the day at the hospital, she just continued with her merry self like she had always done her entire life.

Louise was orphaned at 2 years of age after her mother died giving birth to her seventh or eighth child. Her father took all the boys and raised them as he continued with his business as the local butcher. The girls were each given to relatives.

Mom was given to an aunt who had several much older children. It was the depression and poor Louise spent her childhood running errands and earning her keep. I think she developed her positive disposition in these years. She worked hard and was always cheerful.

Nothing has changed. Even in the face of the worst news, Louise remained calm and cheerful on New Year's Eve.

Hey all you medical specialists who work one-on-one with the dying each and every day with soft spoken voices and gentle eyes, YOU are Canadian. You are VERY CANADIAN.

Chapter 6

A Very Bad Cough

January 2020

New Year's Day, Louise and I rose early to have a cup of coffee and toast. She always played the radio when she ate breakfast. There's something nostalgic about a softly paying radio in the morning.

One of my fondest memories of Mom was when I was a young girl, she would put the radio on after breakfast and after getting my siblings off to school. She would use that time to houseclean or to get dressed to go shopping in downtown Regina. Her favorite song to get ready to was *Downtown* sung by Petula Clark:

> When you're alone and life is making you lonely
> You can always go Downtown
> When you've got worries all the noise and the hurry
> Seems to help I know
> Downtown
>
> (Songwriters: Tony Hatch / James Cauty / Bill Drummond)

Meanwhile, fifty-five years later, here we were puttering around the house and by about 6:00 a.m., I started to get a sore throat. A little brandy and hot water would fix it. I have no time to be sick.

Thinking nothing of it, I did my best to fight this little bug. By the next evening, I had noticed that my condition was worsening. A few nights later, I was convinced that I needed to head to the nearest walk-in clinic.

I thought it was odd that the doctor seemed so nervous when I presented myself to him. "Gee," I thought, "that's really strange how nervous he is around me."

He quickly looked in my throat, gave me a prescription, and ran out of the room. Wow! How odd is that?

Anyway, I was happy to get my prescription and ran to get it filled. Then I headed back to Mom's house. I was sleeping over at her house full time by this point.

When I arrived, I took my medication and went straight to bed. I remember waking up in the middle of the night and thinking that something was not right. I felt so sick – I couldn't breathe! Oh well, just let the medicine kick in. I'm sure I will start feeling better tomorrow.

In the morning, my sister came over. She noticed that I was sick. At the same time, one of my brother's called and heard me hacking in the background. He grunted that the last thing Mom needed is me coughing all over her.

I agreed but no one else could stay overnight to be with her. At this juncture, there was no way she could be left alone. I could never live with myself if I thought for a moment that I would leave her all alone when she is sick and waiting for her biopsy results.

So, we carried on as usual. Like any other night, I prepared a delicious meal for Mom and me and poured us both a glass of wine. We watched the news and Jeopardy.

The news headlines started to emerge that there is a very contagious virus spreading in China and New York – Covid 19.

Well, we're a long way away from both places so I wasn't concerned. A few hours later, I was starting to hit the wall – so to speak. I remember reclining in the easy chair beside Mom in her easy chair. I could not breathe. I thought to myself – Oh my God, I do not think I'm going to make it through the night!

But what could I do? I could not go to the emergency ward because what would I do with Louise. That is the most dangerous place I could take her.

So, I dragged myself into my car at 11 p.m. and drove to the local pharmacy. Barely breathing, I walked up to the pharmacist who was working alone. I said to him, "I can't breathe. I was just at the walk-in clinic and they said it's just a throat infection. Do you have anything to help get me through the night?"

Well, the pharmacist looked at me with the same look of dread as the physician. He literally threw an asthma inhaler at me and said, "Here use this."

I quicky began inhaling from it. Paid him and somehow drove myself back to Louise's house.

I hit the easy chair again. Mom was still watching TV in her chair. I remember looking over at her and seriously thinking, "I don't know who is going to die first. Me or her!"

Reflecting on it all now, I realize that I had Covid 19 and probably caught it at the hospital when Mom when in for her biopsy. I wonder to this day, how many of the patients in that ward died from Covid that month.

Pharmacists who work alone into the late-night hours risking their own lives to help strangers – that's Canadian. That's VERY Canadian.

Chapter 7

Heaven Speaks

January 2020

Mom and I continued to wait to hear about her biopsy results. Meanwhile, normal life continued – at least for a few weeks until all hell broke loose.

At this time in my career, I was both a full-time realtor and a part- time sessional instructor at a local university. I returned to the start of January classes not knowing the storm that was about to begin.

I dragged myself into the university with my "head cold" (LOL) and tried to deliver my lectures as best as I could. There were murmurings that Covid was making its way into Canada.

I started the term teaching in the classroom as any other term before that but before too long announcements were emerging that the government felt it may be unsafe to continue with in class learning.

Meanwhile, Mom got the phone call from her family physician that her results of the biopsy were in. I drove her to the clinic and we met with her family physician. He delivered the news to us that Louise had stage four Pancreatic cancer that had spread to her stomach, exactly the same diagnosis that the doctor had given us just few days before Christmas.

We had prepared ourselves for this inevitable outcome and discussed treatment options. Stage four pancreatic cancer is very unforgiving, especially when it spreads to the stomach. Louise had made it very clear to everyone that cancer treatments were out of the question. She wanted to have a loving peaceful supportive care experience at home or in a palliative care home until her passing, which was estimated to be between three to six months.

My sister, Sandi, got into action and managed to secure a spot for Mom to transition into Foyer Lacombe Palliative Care facility in St. Albert. It had an excellent reputation for delivering excellent palliative care in a loving and supportive environment that included the patient and the family. And it was a Catholic-centered facility, which meant a lot to all of us.

Mom felt very fortunate to secure this spot and we began preparations to move her to the facility. By the end of January, Mom had a private room at Foyer Lacombe and we began our daily visits with her.

As if by fate, no sooner had Mom moved into Foyer Lacombe than her new book, *Revealing the Mysteries of Heaven*, by David Jeremiah, appeared on her doorstep.

I was so excited to visit Mom and start reading to her from this much anticipated book, which she and I had ordered a few weeks earlier.

I arrived just in time for dinner with Mom. The chef at Foyer Lacombe was a wonderful man who really shared his talent with the dying by crafting excellent menus each and every night. We were allowed to bring wine (or other delights) into the facility. So, Mom and I had dinner every night with great food and wine – just like we did at home. It was really marvelous!

"Hey Mom. Guess what?" I asked. "What?" she said. "Our book on heaven has arrived. Look!"

Well, she laughed so hard remembering that funny telemarketing phone call we had had earlier when we told the call center agent that wouldn't be put on a back-order list – we had no time to wait!

"Well, read it to me," Louise said.

Not knowing what to expect, I opened the book to the first chapter, "What's Up with Heaven?"

Dr. Jeremiah begins the book with references to the Bible and how the Bible has a lot to say on the topic of heaven: "Heaven is the most encouraging subject in the Bible and the happiest location in the universe. You should know all about it (p. vii)"

I wasn't sure how interested Louise was in reading passages from the Bible. She was a bit of an enigma when it came to her faith. I knew she believed in God. She converted to Catholicism when she married my father, but one thing was clear – Louise never really enjoyed going to Mass. She always complained that it made her dizzy. I was never clear on whether that was true or just an excuse to not go! Sometimes parents can be a lot like raising a teenager!

One thing was abundantly clear about Louise. She was the closest example of an angel I had ever encountered in my whole life. She protected her children and loved everyone – no exceptions. She had an aura about her of peace and acceptance and everyone who ever met her felt it!

With some trepidation, I began reading Dr. Jeremiah's book:

God has created us for eternity. We are made for heaven - that's our true residence. That's our country. That's our destination. If we do not understand that, and if we do not feed that hunger with the spiritual truth of the Word of God, we end up suppressing that need and replacing it with cheap and tawdry things that will leave us empty and without satisfaction. That's one of the reasons we need to devote ourselves to the study of heaven and set our minds on things above. That's why I've written this book. *(Jeremiah p. 8)*

I looked up to watch Mom's expression. She seemed very peaceful and didn't have much to say except, "Go on."

We both sipped on our Goldschläger Cinnamon Schnapps Liquor with real gold flakes in it and nibbled on our delicious dessert.

Wow this was rich!

Dr. Jeremiah went on to explain that if we want to get into heaven, we must make a reservation!

Well, Louise and I started laughing our heads off at this point. Making reservations was something we knew very well how to do. Afterall, our favorite pastime was eating in restaurants.

"Make a reservation, Sharon. Make a reservation!" she exclaimed.

"Okay, Mom, I will. How about if we put Dr. Jeremiah's book away for today. Would it be okay if we pray a bit together before I head home?" I asked.

"Sure," she said.

Being the reformed Catholic that I am, I pulled out my rosary and began to pray it with Louise. She listened, tried to participate as much as possible and nodded off to sleep.

Home, I went. Back to my real home to prepare myself for teaching the next day.

Hey chefs who work in hospitals and health care institutions. When you try each day to make those meals tasty for the patients, you are being Canadian – THAT'S very Canadian.

Chapter 8

Life is Fun in Palliative Care!

February 2020

I hope the readers don't find the title of this chapter insensitive, but I really mean it – at least from our own personal experience.

Louise was having a grand time at Foyer Lacombe!

First of all, I have to say that the drugs were amazing, and so were the doctors prescribing the drugs. They did a careful assessment of what prescriptions Louise would need to keep the pain at bay. A few days shortly after she was put on morphine, Louise's mood changed considerably. She was funny like all the time. At one point she said to me, "how come I didn't feel this way throughout my life?"

I gotta say, it was a tremendous relief to me that she had adjusted so well to her pain killer and to her new digs.

The nurses monitored her throughout the day, and the nursing assistants did everything in their power to keep Louise comfortable.

Her wish was their command – the whole darn medical team! It was amazing.

In the morning, the nursing assistants would take Mom for a wonderful bath in a very big and deep bathtub. I remember accidentally walking in on one of her morning baths and it was like walking into a spa with incredible fragrances of essential oils in the air and nothing but a big smile on Louise's face.

After the bath, she enjoyed a scrumptious breakfast in her private room. The Chef at Foyer Lacombe was a wonderful man with a big heart. He truly loved his job and always put a lot of thought into each and every meal. He would keep the menus fresh and everything he cooked was absolutely delicious. It wasn't too long into Mom's stay that I figured out – I think this is one of the best restaurants in St. Albert and by golly I wanted to enjoy my meals with Mom. (Of course, I had to pay for my meals.)

After breakfast, a Sasha (St. Albert Sturgeon Hospice Association) volunteer would visit Mom and ask her if she wanted to go the Mass at the chapel. Her answer was always a resounding, "Yes." We would carefully dress her cheerfully in a clean robe, hair and make-up done.

The St. Albert Missionary Oblates of Mary Immaculate Priests resided in an adjoining building to this hospice and they offered Mass nearly everyday in which the patients and their families could attend. As I had mentioned before, Louise was a very virtuous person but not really a daily church goer type. But she loved attending these Masses. They were simple and short, and it was a good excuse to get out of the room for a while.

After Mass, Louise would join several other residents in the library for a rousing sing-a-long with the resident social worker. They always sang the oldies. Louise's favorite was always *How Great Thou Art* and they sang that one each and every time she came:

> Oh Lord, my God
> When I, in awesome wonder
> Consider all the worlds Thy hands have made
> I see the stars, I hear the rolling thunder
> Thy power throughout the universe displayed
> Then sings my soul, my Saviour God to Thee
> How great Thou art, how great Thou art
> Then sings my soul, my Saviour God to Thee
> How great Thou art, how great Thou art
> *Songwriter: Stuart K. Hine*

After sing-a-long, it was back to the room for a bit of rest before lunch. A nurse, doctor, or volunteer would always drop by to see how she was doing. Always cheerful, Louise attracted a fair number of medical personnel who always loved to drop by just to be with her. One nursing assistant told me that whenever she was having a hard day, she would always drop by to visit Louise and the instant she walked into Louise's room, her mood would change from tired and downtrodden to uplifted and cheerful. She told me she always felt her energy come back, and she could finish her day.

Of course, lunch was always delightful. I remember the desserts were delicious. Louise and I would always indulge and finish lunch with a coffee and a shot of Goldschläger – it has "real gold flakes" in it.

Sometimes after lunch, one of the women from the Catholic Women's League would drop by to chat it up with Louise or challenge her to a game of Crib. The loveliest of them all was undoubtedly Rachelle who was in charge of the prayer shawl ministry.

A few volunteers from Holy family Parish would knit prayer shawls and Rachelle was the director of this whole operation. She would hunt for the best wool and knitting material and ensure that the knitters always had a project on the go. The church would house these shawls and whenever anyone was in need of one, Rachelle would pick out just the right shawl and ask our parish priest to bless it. Then she would deliver it to the sick person.

One afternoon, I walked into Louise's room to find a beautiful turquoise shawl on her bed. Mom loved that shawl and she always enjoyed the CWL visits even though she barely knew any of these women.

This hospice was a Catholic sponsored one so there was no shortage of bibles, prayers, hymns, and visitors. One evening, I walked into the hospice, past the Oblate priests who sometimes had dinner in the cafeteria. They were always so welcoming. They waved to me and asked how I was doing. I walked over to their table and told them that Louise was doing very well. She has been extremely well treated and is at peace. But would one of them mind giving her the Sacrament of Sick sometime soon?

One of the priests said he would come by directly after dinner. He was very congenial and I knew Louise would love a visit from him. If my memory serves me correctly, I believe this wonderful priest's name was Father Louis-Philippe Roy. I remember that because he made a joke that Louise and him have the same name.

Mom liked this priest very much right from the get go. They were from the same generation and they seemed to understand each other. With a very gentle voice, Fr. Louis asked mom, "Would you like to confess any sins?" At this point, I felt quite uncomfortable being the room and asked them if they would like me to leave. There was no time for anyone to answer as Louise answered, "No," quite quickly. Fr. Louis brought out his Holy Water and administered the sacrament for the sick.

A sacrament is a visible sign of an invisible aspect of Christ's salvation (Cathechism, 774). The Anointing of the Sick grants onto the sick person a grace, given by Christ, to heal or transform the person. Sacraments are extraordinarily powerful and they can have the effect of enabling the recipient to partake of divine nature (Cathecism. 1129).

Fr. Louis prayed over Louise and then anointed her with Holy oil. This sacrament can strengthen or heal the recipient or give them peace and courage to face their illness. It is a gift of the Holy

Spirit and can renew the person's trust and faith in God (Cathechism, 1520) In other words, it has the potential to heal the body and or soul.

Most importantly, this sacrament completes our journey on earth and prepares our way to our heavenly home with Christ. Do it, arrange it for your loved ones. It gave both Louise and I tremendous peace and as you read later in this book, prepared her to pass over to eternal life.

Life carried on in Foyer Lacombe, Louise's new home. She was so very happy and had the best medical care. Pain was not even in her vocabulary – only wine selection, food choices, and visitor stories.

She had never had so much Catholicism in her daily routine as she had now and she was loving it. Every evening, I continued reading from her newest, favorite book, *Revealing the Mysteries of Heaven* by David Jeremiah. Dr. Jeremiah is not Catholic; he is an Evangelical author and senior pastor of a South Baptist megachurch in San Diego. She loved his book and she loved talking about heaven.

Louise had lots of questions about heaven and I knew none of the answers. I went out of my way to find a popular Catholic-based book that explains it but I couldn't find one. Dr. Jeremiah's book found us and so I had no reason to reject it. We read on: "God has placed within your heart a hunger for eternity, a hunger for heaven, and a yearning for everlasting life (p. 7)."

Dr. Jeremiah wrote on that many churches neglect the topic of heaven. I began wondering if the Catholic Church was one of them? Do not get me wrong. I am not about to start bashing my own church but I was beginning to wonder why I had attended Mass nearly every day for twenty years and can tell you almost nothing about heaven! My curiosity was peaked and more importantly, so was Louise's and that is all that counted at this moment so we continued reading.

The word *heaven* is mentioned more than 500 times in the Bible. Thirty three of the thirty-nine Old Testament books talk about heaven, along with twenty-one books in the New Testament. In the Old Testament, the primary Hebrew term is *shamayim*, which is a plural word meaning "the heights." The New Testament uses the Greek word *Ouranos*, which inspires the name of the plane Uranus. The word refers to something that is raised up, or lofty. So the language of the Bible speaks of heaven as a place that is high and lofty and lifted up. (Jeremiah, p. 9)

Dr. Jeremiah went on to explain that heaven plays such an important role in the Bible that if you deleted all of its references, the text of the Bible would just fall apart in key places turning it into mishmash.

These words screamed out at me from the pages of his book almost as a foreshadowing of what was about to happen - not just to our little hospice in St. Albert, AB, but the entire world. Louise was clearly seated in palliative care heaven and no one could have foreseen how that was about to become a horrible mishmash with the unraveling of everything "love" and "spiritual" operating within it. A head on collision with a world-wide pandemic was on its way, and we were directly in its path.

Watching the news had always been our evening ritual and so I put the book down and Louise and I turned on the TV to listen to the nightly news. We had heard about COVID-19 in China and in the United States but it seemed to hit Canada in one day, March 12th, when the Prime Minister's wife, Sophie tested positive for Covid-19, the NHL suspended its season, the Juno Awards were shelved, the Minor Hockey league across Canada suspended its season, and the Ontario government decided to close schools for two weeks after the March break.

I was still teaching at the university and so the first thought that entered my mind was if our classes would go strictly online. Beyond that, I had never imagined the catastrophe heading our way.

To religious leaders who give up their evening hours to visit the dying – that's Canadian – that's very Canadian.

Chapter 9

Paradise Continued

March 2020

The next morning, I went to visit Louise and the same routine began all over again. That was fine with us!

It was March 17th – St. Patrick's Day - and we decorated Louise's room with everything green. Mom had breakfast, a bath, and attended Mass. This time I decided to bring in one of my beautiful rabbits for her to hold. Palliative Care is like that – it's a more holistic way to care for the dying and animals have been known to raise the patients' morale.

So, I walked in with a black carrying case and a cute little creature named Pearl housed within it. Pearl was a very gentle and timid rabbit who loved to be cuddled. She was white with a giant black mustache! I always thought she looked like some kid just took a black sharpie and drew a thick line between her nose and mouth. Because she took herself quite seriously, we always called her the Princess, which just added to the humor of Pearl's appearance.

The hospice volunteer ensured Pearl could be a visitor and then she accompanied us to mom's room. Mom was delighted when I took Pearl out of the carrying case and placed her on Mom's chest. Pearl enjoyed the visit too. After a short visit, I returned Pearl to her case and carried her home.

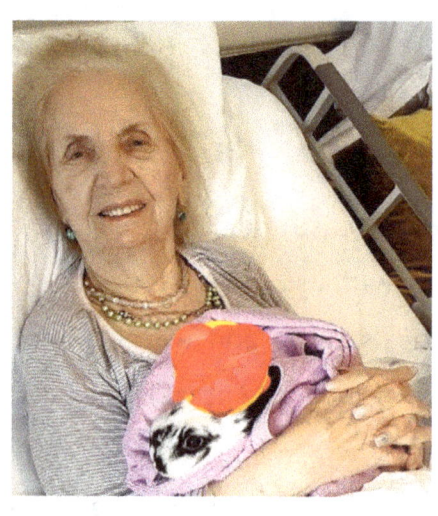

When another visitor heard that we could take pets in to see Louise, she followed suit and brought her lap dog who was known to have a bit of an attitude. The visitor walked the dog through the hallway to Louise's room when no sooner he pooped all over the floor.

The nurses had to include poop scooping onto their list of duties that morning and they were not impressed. By the very next day, an announcement went out that pets were no longer allowed at Foyer Lacombe. Who could blame them?

The afternoon was filled with a steady stream of visitors – all dressed in green. Mom's room looked like a theme room at a hotel! Balloons, streamers, cards, presents in gift bags, wine and liquor bottles lining her walls, a gorgeous floor lamp brought from her home, loads of quilts and pillows, books, magazines, and flowers. She was having a ball!

When the dust settled and the visitors left, Mom and I had a quiet dinner with wine while watching the evening news.

Alberta had just declared a state of emergency and Canada announced it was closing its borders to non-Canadians, except for Americans.

The university classes I were teaching went from face-to-face learning in the classroom to online learning. In an instant, I had to adapt to online learning with four large sections of students and very little to no training on the new platform. It was the last thing I needed at this juncture in my life while I was attending to my dying mother, thriving in my real estate career, and now trying desperately to deliver online lectures with few people I could call for help.

I was not about to abandon my precious visitor hours with Mom. In fact, I ramped up my search for ways to expand our conversations about heaven. I continued to read from Dr. Jeremiah's book, *Revealing the Mysteries of Heaven*, but also included the Divine Mercy Chaplet by Saint Faustina, a Polish nun.

Catholics acknowledge the existence of heaven as do most other religions. We call the people who make it into heaven saints.

Catholics believe those who reach perfection will enter heaven: "So be perfect, just as your heavenly Father is perfect (Mt 5:48)."

Saints are those people who made it into heaven. They achieved perfection. To achieve perfection, one must do the will of God, devote oneself to the glory of God, and love and serve one's neighbor. *Love* being the operative word. God is love.

Saint Faustina had a special mission. This humble Polish nun was a mystic and she had many visions of Jesus. In one vision, Jesus appeared to her with two rays of light emanating from his heart – one red and one pale. The red ray represents the Blood of Christ (the new covenant) and the pale ray represents water, which represent baptism.

The Catholic Church has seven sacraments that members can partake of. Sacraments are a visible sign of invisible grace of God. They are "the masterworks of God." The purpose of the sacraments is to sanctify people. They impart upon the recipient the grace that they signify. For example, the sacrament of Baptism signifies the Christian being reborn as a son/daughter of God. The sacrament of penance and reconciliation confers upon the recipient pardon from God for the offence committed. The sacrament of the sick is designed to strengthen those who are ill and that the Lord will raise him/her up and forgive his/her sins.

In fact, there are seven sacraments: baptism, confirmation, eucharist, penance, sick, holy orders, and matrimony.

The gist of it all is that Christ promises eternal salvation to all souls who trust in his mercy. The two rays of light emanating from his chest represent the Holy Sacraments and all the graces conferred onto the person by the Holy Spirit. The correct disposition of a person receiving these graces is faith and trust in God's mercy. He said to Saint Faustina:

"Today I am sending you with My mercy to the people of the whole world. I do not want to punish aching mankind, but I desire to heal it, pressing it to My merciful Heart' (Diary, 1588).

"... make known to souls the great mercy that I have for them, and to exhort them to trust in the bottomless depths of My mercy" (Diary, 1567).

He told her to paint the image and to have the words "Jesus, I trust in You" printed below.

Most importantly, Jesus said to Saint Faustina:

"By means of this Image I shall be granting many graces to souls; so let every soul have access to it" (Diary, 570)

"LET EVERY SOULD HAVE ACCESS TO IT???"" Really?! I said to myself. Well then, if Mom is truly curious about heaven and she has a very short amount of time left on this earth, then why don't I just trust in everything Jesus imparted to Saint Faustina onto Mom!

We have nothing to lose. Let's just go on faith and trust alone, follow Jesus' instructions and see what happens?

And that's exactly what we did. And the result was simply unimaginable!

Jesus gave Saint Faustina a short Chaplet to accompany the image. The chaplet is called *The Chaplet of the Divine Mercy*. It is short (compared to a rosary) and can be said in its entirety in about seven minutes! The purpose of the chaplet is to obtain mercy for oneself or others, to trust in Christ's mercy, and to show mercy to others. (See Appendix A for the entire Chaplet of Divine Mercy).

Christ told Saint Faustina:

"I promise that the soul that will venerate this image will not perish. I also promise victory over its enemies already here on earth, especially at the hour of death, I myself will defend it as My own glory." (Diary, 48)

God promises that every soul that recites the Chaplet of Divine Mercy at their hour of death, God will pardon them and grant them unfathomable mercy and defend them as if He were defending His own glory. Wow!

"At the hour of death, I defend as My own glory every soul that will say this chaplet; or when others say it for a dying person, the pardon is the same. When this chaplet is said by the beside of a dying person, God's anger is placated, unfathomable mercy envelops the soul, and the very depths of My tender mercy are moved for the sake of the sorrowful Passion of My son." (Diary, 811)

Now the reader may be asking, "Ya but what if the dying person can't recite the Chaplet of Divine Mercy or doesn't even know about this Chaplet. Can he/she still be granted pardon from all their sins and obtain God's mercy."

Yes! Jesus said to St. Faustina (see previous quote) that He will grant pardon to anyone to whom the Chaplet of Divine Mercy was recited for at the hour of death. Now St. Faustina writes about her many experiences with dying and noted that in many instances she wasn't at their bedside at their exact hour of death but learned later that they died pretty close to her last visit.

Furthermore, she notes that she would recite this chaplet from a distance for the dying person and learn that they had died peacefully.

In other words, Jesus told St. Faustina that a person can recite this chaplet for themselves when they are close to their death or someone can recite it for them either in person or from afar and he would still grant the dying person complete pardon and defend them as His own glory.

Well, all of that really shook my world. I took these words very seriously and made a conscious effort to just have faith that what Jesus told St. Faustina was real and that He meant it.

Besides, we had nothing to lose, so I began reciting the Chaplet of Divine Mercy to Mom.

At first, I did not know how she would respond to my praying with her in her room but the chaplet is only seven minutes long and Louise loved it. So, pray I did, each and every day!

To all people who pray on behalf of their loved ones and the dying, THAT'S CANADIAN. That's VERY Canadian.

Chapter 10

Paradise Lost: Locked Out!

March 2020

March 17, 2020, our St. Patrick's Day party was our last big hurrah. I continued to visit mom for breakfast and dinner and we would watch history unfold on the national news each night. Little did we know that in just a few short weeks, we would be the top story on the national news.

On March 18, 2020, Canada and the United States closed their borders to non-essential traffic, and more provinces declared a state of emergency.

All non-essential staff were told to work from home. Restaurants, hair salons, and movie theatres were closing their doors.

People ran to Costco and bought out every package of toilet paper.

As for my real estate practice, I was in complete shock that the government declared realtors ESSENTIAL workers! Wow! Who would have thought?

I'm an essential worker. We were allowed to continue listing and selling homes because housing was considered an essential trade.

Because I sell not only residential homes but also businesses, I had several restaurant listings in March 2020, and watched with horror as the value of these business dropped by over 75%. Many restaurant owners secured their leases with their principle residences and so if their business failed, they would also lose their home.

The federal government stepped up with emergency loans and wage subsidy programs. This program saved nearly all the restaurants from going out of business. But this industry was shaken right to the core.

I witnessed restaurant owners lose their livelihood and some marriages were disintegrated in the process.

So much pain.

So real estate continued with my business listings put in triage and on life support with an urgent necessity to find buyers.

My university classes were all put online in an instant and there was no time for instructors to learn new platforms. Students were outraged by the sudden lack of service.

And then just when I thought things could not get worse, the worst of everything happened.

Foyer Lacombe announced a strict visitor protocol of one visitor per day per patient. My job was to schedule family members in to see Mom in a fair and equitable manner. We managed okay although there was evidence Mom was experiencing loneliness with the decreased visits.

Simultaneously, my daughter was giving birth in a local hospital and visitors were not permitted. I had only two family members in my life at that time – my mother and my daughter. And I was restricted in visiting both of them at the same time. One dying and the other giving birth to my first grandchild.

Mom was starting to feel the strain of reduced visitations. On April 5th, I sent this text to my siblings:

"Just spoke with Mom. She is OUT OF IT.

The nurse is feeding her. She seems completely non understanding of why she has been abandoned. That much she DOES get. I urge any of you to call her now while the nurse is there to help her answer the phone. Your heart will break."

I thought to myself that perhaps I should bring her home to my place. At least she will be comfortable and we can all visit her as often as we want.

I made my case to Foyer Lacombe and they turned me down. She needed more advanced medical care than I could give her.

That was enough to break my heart and then the unthinkable happened.

On April 4, 2020, early in the morning, I went for my breakfast visit with mom and found that the doors to Foyer Lacombe had been locked. I tried to pull them open when a nurse and the director of Foyer Lacombe came out to tell me that the government had issued a lock-out order prohibiting anyone from entering the facility unless the patient was "actively dying."

"Actively dying" means they have about two hours left to live. By the way, that's exactly when I don't want to be present. Have you ever seen anyone who is actively dying. It's not a pretty sight and I wanted to remember my mom when she was in a calm state – like now!

When the nurses delivered the news to me, I collapsed onto a park bench and could not hold myself up. I couldn't speak. All I could do was shake my head. "No. No." I said to myself, "You don't have the right to do this."

It was at that moment that I knew my fight was about to become political – and it did!

Health care leaders who think it's okay to prevent the dying from being with their loved one - That's NOT Canadian.

Chapter 11

The Sound of Silence

April 2020

The lockout order meant that all visitors were prohibited from visiting their loved ones, all volunteers were prohibited from working in the palliative care wards, and the remaining nurses and nurse assistants were left to covered for all those duties those people did.

The soul was stripped right out of these palliative care wards, hospital wards, and seniors' care centres. Visitors and volunteers regularly fed those patients, washed those patients, brushed their hair, and prayed with them. The nurses and nursing aids were left to fill in the gaps and did the best they could. But their time was more than used up administering medications, changing beds, and feeding patients.

Coupled with that the nurses had to organize zoom calls with family members, which must have drove them up the wall. We had four siblings, four grandchildren, and five great grandchildren to accommodate with zoom calls and that was just for one patient. Imagine what those nurses had to endure ensuring each patient had sufficient social time on zoom to prevent them from diving into a deep depression.

The whole scene was completely insane. We had arranged for "window visits" with our dying relatives. This involved the family deciding who would get the precious "window" time and when, then notifying the nurses who then had to ensure that each patient was dressed and sitting upright and close enough to the window to be able to make out the silhouettes of relatives waving at them through the glass. Considering these patients were near death and on serious medications like morphine, etc., you can only imagine how ludicrous this whole arrangement had become.

Personally, I went from feeding Mom breakfast and dinner and praying with her every night to tapping on the window trying to get her attention and desperately watching her stare of confusion and loneliness as she tried to figure out what was going on.

I remember driving my car to her window and taking a lawn chair out from my trunk and camping outside her window waiting anxiously for the nursing aides to raise the blinds so I could wave at her. The nursing aides always did a remarkable job of getting her dressed in her best clothes and combing her hair. They would sit her in a chair near the window and she always looked so beautiful. I thank those nursing aides profusely for their dedication.

As I was sitting in my lawn chair, I would always say high to the relative of the patient in the next room who would also be camped outside their relative's window. Naturally, we developed a bit of a kinship. Often, we would camp for a very long time just waiting for our loved one to open their eyes and hopefully recognize who we were.

I knew that mom was disturbed by the isolation she was experiencing. She was in a private room and suddenly found herself completely alone – all day and all night. No more parties, no more hand massages, no more hair does, no more prayers.

I was most angry with how this lock out order stripped these patients from their right to practice their religion at a time in their lives when they needed it most. I was angry with all the silence I had to endure – silence in the churches, silence in the classrooms, silence in the restaurants, and silence at my dying mother's window as she was too weak to talk through the glass.

I remember that at this time, Easter was approaching and it was on Good Friday when yet again there I sat completely alone praying the rosary through the window for my mom. The priests were instructed to close their churches.

The parallel between my situation and that of Mary Magdalene who was the only one who ran to the tomb to visit Jesus' dead body. The apostles were afraid for their life and remained locked up in the upper room. It was a woman who ran to visit the tomb and it was largely women who remained to care for the dying and pray for the dying.

This pandemic stripped our country of its most essential values and was tantamount to the crucifixion of humanity. Never did I imagine that Canadians would abandon their seniors and dying family members because the government issued lock out orders. Never did I imagine that the priests of my church would be locked out of their churches and ordered to remain within their rectories, leaving us abandoned in parking lots praying to God for mercy through window panes of our dying relatives isolated rooms.

My mind could not absorb all the levels of betrayal taking place. I imagined myself breaking through the door of the ward and running past the nurses to my mother's room. Arrest me. I don't care. You have taken away the religious freedom of my family and I will show you that that was an error in leadership from behind prison walls if necessary.

I decided to start fighting back. I had made numerous calls to the nursing staff at Foyer Lacombe but they had no power and I did not want to distract them from their nursing duties. So, I quickly abandoned that tactic and began writing letters to senior directors at Alberta Health Services.

I had had numerous phone calls with government people including ombudsmen, government directors, and the director of Foyer Lacombe. In an attempt to appease me, they had arranged a conference call with several directors from Alberta Health Services who worked directly with Dr. Hinshaw, staff from Foyer Lacombe, an ombudsman, one of my siblings and me.

The call began with a very compassionate tone. They acknowledged their understanding of how painful this situation was for us and took turns providing us with a detailed explanation of the rules, the lock-out order, why the lock-out order was necessary, and steps going forward.

I remained completely silent throughout the call and listened carefully to their explanations. At one point, one of the doctors explained in detail how viruses work and how they need to protect the health of the residents first and foremost and that is why I could not see my mom, "So you see, Sharon, why we can't let you visit your mother?"

My mind was racing at turbo speed trying to figure out what I should say. I knew I could not win the science argument. I believed that with PPE they could allow visitors in and keep patients safe but they argued that providing PPE for all the visitors would be too expensive.

In fact, there were only 66 palliative care beds in Alberta. A set of PPE costs about $7. If every patient gets two visitors per week and they only have two months to live, the total cost to the government is only $7392.00. Even if my math if off ... it's not a lot of money.

I decided not to use that argument because they would surely have a quick rebuttal and that would be the end of our call. So, I paused for what felt like a thousand years but was only about six seconds. That six seconds was the loudest sound of silence that I had felt throughout this whole ordeal and then the words slowly came out of my mouth: "That's not Canadian," I said.

"It's not Canadian that we abandon our seniors and dying family members in Canada. Even terrorists have more rights than that. The United National Declaration of Human Rights, Article 5, states that no one has the right to inflict torture or subject another human to cruel or inhuman treatment. Isolating seniors and the dying in the final weeks of life is torture and inhuman."

Although the government had to legal right to impose these lock-out orders, they overstepped their ethical right to do so. Article 30 of the United Nations Declaration of Human Rights states that "no government, group or individual should act in a way that would destroy the rights and freedoms of the Universal Declaration of Human Rights."

The entire conference call when dead silent and I felt at that moment that you could hear a pin drop out there in the universe. That was the loudest sound of silence I had ever heard.

Then one of the officials said in a very gentle voice, "Sharon, we will take steps to ensure you and your family have communication with your mother. A nurse from Foyer Lacombe will call you later today to set up a schedule for phone calls, zoom visits, and window visits."

And they did. And we did – we continued our window visits and phone calls but my fight had only just begun. This was not the end. It was only the beginning.

Subjecting seniors and dying people to isolation is cruel and inhuman treatment tantamount to torture and THAT'S NOT CANADIAN.

Chapter 12

Calling in the Big Guns

April 2020

News was starting to break that long term care homes in Ontario were experiencing abhorrent living conditions. The toxic combination of visitor locked-outs and staff shortages made for a very potent and deadly cocktail of resident neglect leading to horrifying deaths – and not from Covid.

Bed ridden seniors were left to fend for themselves and unable to get food or water. The homes were infested with cockroaches and bugs, fecal contamination was found on the walls of residents and within their own fingernails. Patients would cry for help with no staff responding.

Eventually the government sent in the military to pick up the pieces, and they confirmed and reported these abhorrent conditions. Many residents died of dehydration.

Meanwhile back in St. Albert, we remained locked out of Foyer Lacombe but I felt the residents still had good nursing care. Nevertheless, watching my mother's mental health deteriorate before my eyes in a matter of days had me working in overdrive to win back our visitation rights.

I tried the diplomatic route and had made my appeal to the director of the facility, Alberta Health Services directors, and leaders of the Catholic Church. (See letters at end of this chapter).

I know mom was feeling abandoned because whenever she spoke to me on the phone, she would say, "Why won't you visit me?" Sickening.

Essentially, this was a political problem. At the heart of the issue was the fact that none of the politicians wanted to die on this ant hill. If they allowed visitors into palliative care wards and outbreaks occurred resulting in mass deaths, they would be condemned for allowing visitors into the facilities.

Then I spoke with a politician who was very experienced about the matter. He indicated to me that behind closed doors, the government officials discussed the strategy of denying visitation rights until the public protested – then they would think more creatively about how to allow visitors in to see their dying loved ones.

Once I had learned about their line of reasoning, I knew my fight had a new purpose and a chance of a positive outcome if I could only begin a public protest in defense of visitation rights.

I reached out to all the family members I had met during the parking lot visits and proposed a media event whereby we would call the press at a time when all the parking lot families would be visiting their dying relatives. We would set up chairs all along the windows of the facility looking into our relatives' room, and we would all be wearing T-shirts that said on the back, "Let Us In!"

I figured this visual would be strong enough to make national news and embarrass our politicians so that they would relinquish and change the lock-out order to enable palliative care patients their visitation rights.

Sadly, no one wanted to participate! At first, I was baffled by everyone's reluctance to create a media storm, but then I had realized that they were afraid of retribution against their loved ones by the internal staff, who might see our story as criticism against them.

Once I had realized the reason for the other families' reluctance to participate, I knew my fight was singular, and so I had to take a different approach.

It was time for a different tactic!

Immediately, I wrote a heartfelt email to my MLA, MP, board of directors of Covenant Health, AND even the POPE!

Yes, I felt that because Foyer Lacombe was a Catholic-based palliative care unit that the Catholic Church had a role to play in helping us earn back the residents' right to practice their religion in their final days of life, and to ensure they had the compassionate care of their loved ones in their final weeks of life.

Simultaneously, I sent "News Flashes" to all the major newspapers in our area. I tried every avenue to get their attention to our fight in St. Albert.

Within hours, the Edmonton Journal called me and wanted to cover our story. We arranged for a photographer to meet me outside my mother's window to witness a window visit. As well, CTV called me and wanted to cover our story on the national news.

My very first thought upon receiving this news was that I could not possibly be the only person in the province experiencing this heart wrenching story. There must be literally hundreds more just like me. But how do I find them?

FACEBOOK, of course! Social media is the perfect tool for this situation. I immediate lowered the security settings on my personal Facebook page to allow any member of the public to find me and send me messages. And it worked. No sooner had the Edmonton Journal put our story on the front page of the newspaper than strangers reached out to me to tell me their stories. That was exactly what I needed to turn this into a political battle.

On April 15th, 2020, an Edmonton Journal photographer came with me to Mom's window. The nursing aid handed Mom a phone and they called me on my cell phone. I stood outside her window waving and talking to her on the phone. She was confused by the double communication and continued to talk but seemed unable to see me outside the window.

Nevertheless, we continued our conversation and at one point her voice became very soft and she whispered into the phone, "Sharon," (long pause) "There's a shortage of nurses here."

My heart fell to the ground. OMG, I could not bear to think that my own mother would experience neglect of basic care right in front of my eyes and I would be unable to do anything to help her. What if the horrible conditions we heard about happening in Ontario begin happening here too?

I had to put this campaign into overdrive!

The Edmonton Journal published our story on the front cover on April 16th, 2020, and reiterated the government order to lock out all visitors except for those patients who were "dying." I don't know what you would call someone who was residing in a palliative care ward except "dying!"

Yet we could not get in.

AHS deferred the decision to the directors of each facility to make decisions on a case-by-case basis and many of them had decided that the patient had to be "actively dying" in order to see visitors. "Actively dying" – I was told – is defined as the last two hours of life.

My argument was that no one can predict the hour of anyone's death and that these palliative care patients needed their loved ones now as they were facing imminent death.

I argued that it is harsh and cruel treatment to pull the carpet from under these hospice patients with no notice and no opportunity to prepare them for this. All they know is that they have been abandoned by their family.

I also argued that denying Canadians their right to access their religious points of inspiration was a denial of their basic rights to practice their religion as stipulated by the Canadian Constitution. But of course, I knew that those rights could be trumped by the Health Act, which allowed the governments to institute measures to protect public health.

I had made my appeal very clear to AHS, the press, and the Covenant Care – declare ALL HOSPICE patients as "dying" and the whole problem goes away – simple.

My final quote in the Edmonton Journal was as follows:

We don't have time to get caught up in semantics right now. It could take us months to figure that out. If you're in a hospice, you're dying. So everybody who's in a hospice should be permitted basic human rights to have their essential family visitors visit them with screening and PPE.

In addition to the Edmonton Journal story, CTV came to my parking lot visit and interviewed me and put the story on the National News. I looked horrible and was terribly embarrassed and shocked by my appearance. I had no idea that I had become so run down but one of my friends made me feel better when she said that if I didn't look terrible, nobody would believe the intensity of my suffering. How sad and how true.

Denying visitation rights to the dying under any circumstance demonstrates a lack of moral imagination by political leaders and THAT'S NOT CANADIAN.

Sharon Ryan's letter to media outlets

April 10, 2020

"My God. My God. Why have you forsaken me." Mt 27:46

The Minister of Health has locked out all essential visitors from visiting their dying family members who are in palliative care. These hospice patients are different from long term care ones. Palliative care patients are at the end of their life with only weeks left to live. There are very few palliative care beds in Edmonton.

Our family placed our mother in a Catholic-based hospice – Foyer Lacombe in St. Albert – because we believe in the Catholic tenets of compassion and comfort during this most sacred period of a person's life. With mere weeks left in her life, we are prohibited from seeing her, touching her, comforting her.

We understand the importance of taking proper precautions to prevent the spread of Covid 19; however, political and health leaders should have the moral imagination to balance the interest of all stakeholders in society in making critical decisions – like allowing essential family visitors to see their dying family members in the last few weeks of life. The Alberta Minister of Health has instructed these facilities to only allow essential family members to visit during the last few hours of the patients' life. Meanwhile, our mother is wondering why she has been deserted by her family!

Simple precautions like screening visitors and supplying them with personal protective equipment (mask and gloves), and practicing social distancing are low-cost measures to ensure these few families with members caught in palliative care at this time get a dignified passing from this earth. BTW, there are very few palliative care beds in Edmonton.

Especially if the patient is in a faith-based unit – like Foyer Lacombe – where compassion for the dying is a major tenet of the Catholic Church. There are only 10 palliative care beds in Foyer Lacombe. We believe the cost of PPE to equip essential family members and the risk they pose is very small compared to the huge assault on the patients and families spiritually and emotionally as a result of not being able to comfort their dying family members.

This is a moment of truth for the Catholic Church and for our political leaders to demonstrate that they have the wisdom to live up to the values of their constituents – a time to say to society – We value the emotional and spiritual needs of the dying.

Sharon Ryan's Letter to Government Officials and Catholic Leaders

April 10, 2020

Site Administrator
Foyer Lacombe Hospice
1 St. Vital Avenue
St. Albert, AB T8V 1K1

CC: His Holiness, Pope Francis
Most Reverend, Archbishop Smith
Honourable Jason Kenney, Premier of Alberta
Honourable Tyler Shandro, Minister of Health
Honourable Michael Cooper, MP St. Albert-Edmonton
Honourable Dale Nally, MLA Morinville-St. Alberrt
Honourable Marie PreFontaine, MLA St. Albert
Tracy Sopkow – CEO - Covenant Care

SUBJECT: Name of Patient: Louise Ryan
Age: 90 years
Condition: 4th Stage Pancreatic Cancer
Prognosis: 2 to 3 Weeks Left to Live (As at April 7, 2020)
Residence: Foyer Lacombe St. Albert

"I was sick and you visited me." Mt 25:26

On April 4, 2020, nurses at Foyer Lacombe in St. Albert received a mandatory order from Alberta Health Services to stop allowing visitors into the facility due to Covid-19 concerns. They were told to make executive judgement with respect to visitors of those patients who are at "End of Life."

Our family last visited Louise on April 3, 2020. We could not explain to our mother the situation nor say our last goodbyes while she was in a state of mental alertness.

From April 4 – April 7th, we connected with Louise using the phone and facetime. Because of Louise's medications, she forgets information so the restriction of visitor order due to Covid-19 eludes her mind and memory, leaving her confused and feeling abandoned. She repeated asks, "What is happening to me?" "What is happening to me?" "What is happening to me?" (always in a set of three).

Louise is isolated in a room high above ground level by herself so we cannot look through her window and wave. Instead, the nurses indicated they could put her in a wheelchair and bring her to the lobby, from which we can look through the window and wave. However, this plan is not working as the nurses have indicated she is too drowsy to be put into the chair – and so the isolation continues.

On April 7th, I (daughter) phoned Louise at approximately 3:00 p.m. to find her in a tearful and fretful state. She begged me to come visit her. She cried, "Why won't you come visit me?"

Immediately I called the head nurse who went into to speak with Louise. She determined that the Chaplain (who Louise appreciates very much) had visited her and she asked, "What is happening to me?". Etc. etc. etc. We are not finding fault with the

Chaplain – this story serves to illustrate how important family members are at end of life as we should be there to reassure and pray with our mother.

Our request is summarized below:

1. **Louise IS at "end-of-life"** with only weeks left to live. She needs reassurance and prayer with family members present in her room.
2. Phone calls and facetime and waving through the windows does not substitute for physical presence in her room by loved ones. She is not comprehending our presence through the window as her gaze does not project as far and through the glass.
3. **Louise is experiencing severe emotional trauma and feelings of abandonment** as a result of having no family members present in her room.
4. We placed Louise in a Catholic-centered facility because our family are devoted Catholics. The most **pronounced tenet of the Covenant Foundation is compassionate care:**

"Compassionate Care & Programs: physical, **emotional,** social and spiritual care for patients, residents and families."

The AHS website indicates that "In end-of-life situations when there may be a critical need to visit a loved one, visitors with/or without symptoms may be provided with Personal Protective Equipment (PPE) and escorted to and from the room."

Our family is asking for Louise's basic human right to see her essential visitors with PPE.

The Catholic faith emphasizes the compassionate aspect of Christian life. The Catechism of the Catholic Church emphasis in 1503 (Christ the Physician):

Christ's compassion toward the sick. **"I was sick and you visited me." Mt 25:36**

Foyer Lacombe is Catholic-centered hospice funded by the Catholic Covenant Foundation, whose values are: Respect, Transparency, Collaboration, Impact, Integrity and Stewardship (Covenant Foundation Web site). Many of these values have been transgressed when a simple solution is in sight.

Although we understand the seriousness of Covid-19, we believe that allowing Louise to see her essential visitors with Personal Protective Equipment on a periodic basis **as she IS at End-of-Life with only weeks left to live** would not bankrupt the health care system nor put any residents at risk but rather ensure the Catholic Covenant of **COMPASSION for the dying** is upheld. Anything less is a betray of our Faith and of God.

Let's use our moral imaginations to navigate through these troubling times with reasoned measures balancing our duties to ALL stakeholders but most especially the dying plea of a faithful woman who finds herself abandoned.

As it is Lent, let's not forget the words spoken by Jesus as he hung on the cross to die:

My God. My God. Why have you forsaken me? Mt 27:46

As time is of the essence, I am available 24/7 and await your most immediate response. We are requesting Louise Ryan's essential visitors be allowed to visit her with PPE and screening. Please call me at 780-233-6398

Kindest regards

Dr. Sharon Ryan

Dr. Sharon Ryan
Daughter of Louise Ryan

Chapter 13

A Very Canadian MLA and a Premier with Wisdom

April 2020

I was now in a desperate situation. Mom was deteriorating emotionally and physically right in front of my eyes behind a pane of glass, which I could not penetrate.

My appeals to the higher ups went without notice; so, I did what any woman in my circumstance would do – call Michael Cooper, MP Extraordinaire!

Michael Cooper is perhaps the most interesting MP to come along in Canada for a very long time. He is a young (former) lawyer who became a conservative MP in St. Albert, where I live. He keeps getting re-elected ('15, '19, '21) because the citizens absolutely love this guy.

Michael has been instrumental in legislative reform involving the rights of the dying, where he has fought against physician-assisted dying. He brought to fruition the Juror Mental Health Bill that gives jurors the right to seek therapy, if they need to do so after serving as a juror. Something about this MP is different. He actually has a moral compass and effects change in Canadian law to reflect the values of Canadians.

So, I called Michael Cooper. He answered his phone. I told him about my plight. He spoke with absolute clarity that health matters are not federal jurisdiction and so he couldn't help me directly but he advised me to call my MLA, Dale Nally, because health matters are a provincial jurisdiction. He said that he would talk to Dale about my mother's dilemma and encourage him to help me.

I had made a very emotional appeal for help to my MLA, Honourable Dale Nally. I called his constitution office and spoke with his executive assistant. She empathized with my situation and indicated that she would pass my appeal onto Dale.

A few days after the Edmonton Journal story broke, I got a call from Dale himself: "Sharon, it's Dale Nally. Did you get in to see your mother?"

"No," I replied.

"And," I continued, "I have received a few stories from other Albertans who are experiencing the same grief as me and my family. May I read you a couple of these stories?"

"Sure." Dale replied.

"Well, the saddest one I have is of a ninety-six-year-old woman who has been married to her husband for over seventy-five years. They have never spent a single day apart from each other. Suddenly, her palliative care facility locked-out all visitors including her husband. Now he finds himself humiliated as he sits at her window waving to her. She cannot even see him and he cries."

"Oh," Dale replied, "that is very, very sad."

"Yes," I said. "And there is another one. A middle-aged man is dying in a hospice alone. His parents, aunts, and uncles have travelled a long way by car to visit him and say goodbye. The day they arrived, they were locked-out and unable to say their last goodbyes. He died alone."

"Wow, Sharon," Dale said. "Tomorrow we are having a caucus meeting and the Premier will be there. Can I read these stories to him?"

"Yes," I said, "But do not reveal the identities of the families. They asked me specifically not to mention their names and I want to honor their requests."

"No problem, Sharon. I will follow-up with you after our meeting tomorrow," he said.

Well, that was the longest 24 hours of my life! But sure enough, 24 hours later, I got a phone call from Dale.

Dr. Hindshaw had heard the stories and decided to change the visitation lock-out orders.

Dale continued, "It will take a few days for Dr. Hinshaw to come up with appropriate visitation rules to accommodate visitors but she is working on it and you should be able to get in this week."

Wow. I could not believe my ears. I simply could not believe what I had just heard. It was just unbelievable.

The next day, I got this text from Dale:

I spoke to Dr Hinshaw last night. They wrote the order yesterday and will announce it at her briefing this afternoon. 😊

A day later, on Tuesday, April 28th, 2020, Dr. Hinshaw issued a revised order pertaining to visitation rights of nursing homes and palliative care facilities. In short, she said in her news announcement that they had "heard our stories" and felt it necessary to allow visitors to see residents of nursing homes and palliative care facilities with some restrictions (see Appendix A for copy of the Order):

1. Outdoor visits permitted with one designated essential visitor and one other person while observing social distancing requirements.
2. Indoor visits permitted for one essential visitor only if the resident has been declared as dying.

Before this order, there was no consensus among the operators as to what constituted "dying." Now Dr. Hinshaw had made it clear that it would need to be declared by the medical professionals that the resident had two weeks left to live or less.

That seems harsh but it was much better than the 24 hours left to live declared by some operators.

And remember that we were now entitled to outdoor visits in the meantime and the patients certainly would appreciate getting outside so all in all, we were somewhat satisfied with this new order.

I was declared as the essential visitor by the family and so my next area of emphasis was ensuring everyone had equal visitation rights.

We navigated through that maze quite well and Mom really enjoyed our outdoor visits.

MLAs and MPs who take the time to listen to their constituents' concerns about legal rights are Canadian – they are VERY CANADIAN.

Chapter 14

Paradise Restored: "I'm In!"

April 2020

On April 28th, 2020, Alberta Health Services revised the "visitor lock-out policy" to allow patients to have outdoor visits.

It was an amazing time. The spring weather was glorious with trees and flowers in bloom and birds' chirping filling the air.

We arranged for me and alternative family members to meet Mom outside in the gardens of Foyer Lacombe. The nurses were heroic in accommodating all the patients and their families. It was a herculean task to get these palliative care patients out of bed and dressed so they could present themselves with some degree of dignity to their families and friends.

I remember our first visit; we were all giddy just sitting around in a circle chatting with each other. The gentle breeze on all our faces but most especially on Louise's was an exquisite grace from the heavens. She squinted with the sunlight in her eyes and smiled and relaxed.

I can only imagine how refreshing these visits were for the patients as many of them had not seen the sun or smelled the fresh flowers since they were admitted!

As for me, it felt like I was taking off a tight shoe and breathing a great big sigh of relief. This is everything any of us ever needed – just to sit with each other in a natural setting and to let the healing power of nature overtake our souls in our little circle of love.

This is dying with dignity. Immersing ourselves in the gentle and soft hand of mother nature, having the presence of loved one's envelope us, and sharing the same air with the very persons who gave us life, nurtured us through our childhoods and now are preparing to leave us – albeit temporarily as life is eternal.

I remember mom truly enjoying her outdoor visits and then at some point nodding off to sleep or shivering despite the hot temperatures. We would call the nurse who would wheel sleeping Louise back to her cocoon until the next visit.

I loved these outdoor visits but their frequency was restricted for obvious reasons. The sheer amount of work needed to arrange them by the staff was simply as much as they could take. Volunteers were still restricted so the facilities relied upon the current staff to carry this heavy load.

The key was for our family to win back Louise's right to have an inside visitor as well. That would increase the frequency of visits and help to keep her comforted more often.

Hinshaw's new visitation order stipulated that one essential visitor could get indoor visits if the patient was declared to have two weeks left to live; so, my next task was to ask the doctors to monitor her health.

I did not even have time to start the next leg of my fight to win back mom's visitation rights. Shortly after the patients were awarded outdoor visits, I got a call from Mom's doctor at Foyer Lacombe.

"Sharon, I have evaluated your mother's condition and believe that she may have about two weeks left. I'm going to write my conclusion in her file and ensure you get indoor visiting rights right away."

I was so happy. Can you imagine being happy at news like that? In normal times, that would be sick but these were anything but normal times.

I texted my family members right away and everyone was so relieved to know that mom could have both outdoor and indoor visits.

I remember walking into her room for the first time since the lock-out and feeling completely enveloped with love. Mom was wide awake, happy, and comfortable. The sun was shining through her window. The nurses were coming and going doing their morning routine and all seemed well again!

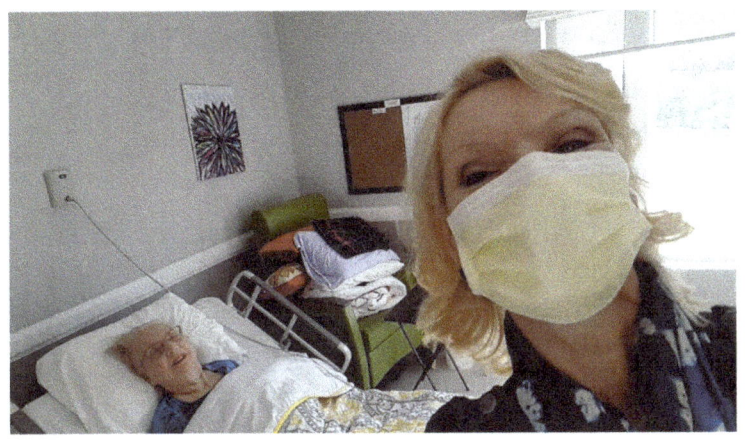

They had stipulations for indoor visitors. We had to be screened for signs of illness, robed from head to toe in PPE, and stay several feet away from the patient.

This quickly became a game of cat and mouse. I was so excited to see Mom and could barely stop myself from hugging her. The nurses would poke their heads in the room as they walked by to ensure I was abiding by the new rules.

When they passed by, I would quickly hug mom and then distance myself from her and then see another nurse pass by to check on me!

I gave more hugs to mom during those visits that at any other time in my life. She must have wondered what the heck was wrong with me. Hug, run away, hug, run away, etc.

One of the first things I did when I got back inside was resume our journey on reading about heaven. Dr. Jeremiah's book, *Revealing the Mysteries of Heaven*, was still on Mom's end table. I picked it up and began reading to her from where we left off, which was just in the middle of chapter 1:

Heaven is a place, a literal location. Jesus said:

> "Let not your heart be troubled; you believe in God, believe also in Me. In My Father's house are many mansions; if it were not so, I would have told you. I go to prepare a place for you. And if I go and prepare a place for you, I will come again and receive you to Myself; that where I am, there you may be also." *(John 14:1-3)*

Mom smiled when I said, "Mom, it says here that heaven is a place – an actual place."

I continued to pray the Divine Mercy Chaplet to Mom because Catholics believe that "when this chaplet is said by the bedside of a dying person, God's anger is placated, unfathomable mercy envelops the soul (Diary, 811)."

Jesus said to St. Faustina: "It pleases Me to grant everything they ask of Me by saying this chaplet" (Diary, 1541) provided that what you ask for is compatible with God's will.

Now for unbelievers, all this may sound like magical fantasy. I get that. As for me, I had made the decision in my later thirties after two decades of pure hell to start a new life, and although I was born into a Catholic family, raised Catholic, I veered away from the Church and into the New Age movement in my late teens.

That did not work out so well for me so in my 37th year of my life, after having a complete breakdown during a divorce, I had made the decision to go for broke and simply just surrender back into my Catholic faith. Along the way, many of the doctrines and practices of devotion took me by surprise but I stuck to my promise to God and to myself that I am all in.

Learning of St. Faustina's mystical experiences with Christ and the resultant Divine Mercy Chaplet was one of the most mystifying experiences in my journey.

Jesus basically told this nun that anyone who prays this Chaplet of Divine Mercy by the bedside of the dying person will placate God's anger and: "The souls that say this chaplet will be embraced by My mercy during their lifetime and especially at the hour of their death" (Diary, 754).

On the not so nice side, He also said to this nun that souls who do not "adore My mercy, they will perish for all eternity" (Diary 998).

Yikes! Now that is the part of religion that people do not want to hear.

You know I had seen many a bad day when I veered away from my faith and tried to be free with the New Age movement. Having come back all in, I understand what true freedom looks like.

True freedom is being able to say "Yes" to your creator through your life expression in every moment both good and bad. True freedom is understanding that you were created in the image and likeness of God and everything you try to do in this life will be blessed and amplified by the creator if it is compatible with his will.

True freedom is understanding that we were all born with free will to love our God or to not love our God. The latter is not a recommended course of action for it leads to decisions that actually counteract God's will and results in plans that will inevitably fail.

And true freedom is expressed in our Canadian Constitution whereby every Canadian shall have the right to practice their religion and when the government locked visitors out of palliative care wards, they thwarted the constitutional right of Canadians to practice their religion at their moments of death.

Catholics have a deep and rich faith going back over 2000 years to the times of Christ involving devotions and practices which Christ himself taught. Countries like Canada have a highly cherished democratic history preserving and protecting the rights of its citizens to enjoy their freedom to practice their religion.

I am fully aware that public health trumps our constitutional rights and that the government was within its legal parameter to institute these harsh lock-out orders, isolating seniors and dying people; however, I was on the front line of this pandemic fighting for the rights of our dying citizens to have their constitutional rights reinstated – if possible.

And it *was* possible to grant them visitation rights. The excuses given to me by health authorities were that there was not even enough PPE (personal protective equipment) for the employees at the hospitals and so they sure were not going to go out of their way to provide it for visitors.

I offered to purchase the PPE for the palliative care ward but the authorities quipped that it must be hospital issued PPE.

I also argued that there were only 66 palliative care beds in the entire province of Alberta at the time and that issuing PPE for at least one visitor per patient per week would not break the bank and would preserve Canadians rights to have a family member by their side as they die.

It is moments like these that define us a people. What kind of society are we to let all these people die in isolation locked up and away from their loved ones. How we treat the most vulnerable in our society defines us as a society.

These were heartless and ruthless decisions based upon convenience and lowest risk for the leaders. It was far easier for them to have a blanket decision to just lock everyone out of these wards than to try to come up with creative alternatives like outdoor visits – how hard was that to dream up!

Many people have told me that the government was trying to protect the life of these palliative care patients and that they had no other choice but to isolate them because no one knew the full capacity of the Covid virus.

I maintain that some attempt to ascertain the risk tolerance of each palliative care patient should have been pursued. It is far too a crucial matter to decide how people living in a democracy will die – alone or with loved ones.

Anyhow, my journey became one of ensuring my mother's passing was a dignified one and now that I was back in the room, I had leverage to play a hand in that – and play it I did.

Leaders who make decisions that hurt the most vulnerable to reduce the risk to their political careers is NOT CANADIAN.

Chapter 15

A Passing into a New Life

July 2020

I was very happy for myself but I needed to get my siblings inside this palliative care ward too. Fortunately for everyone involved, they preferred the outdoor visits so my fighting and begging days were finally over.

We were in a peaceful place with the restrictions and Mom's needs. I retired my political hat and just wanted to be a daughter to Louise in these final weeks.

I have to say that this palliative care ward had amazing doctors, nurses, and nursing aides. Mom's pain was under control and Mom was in a happy place. She continued to enjoy meals, taking herbal baths, and having foot massages. She was always properly bathed and dressed. She always looked beautiful.

God has a special place prepared for health care workers who attend to the dying. These are very special people with extraordinary hearts.

I enjoyed four weeks of indoor visits with Mom before she passed away. That was such a gift from God as she lived one month longer than anticipated.

Her final evening was hard to take. Anyone who has even been by the bedside of a loved one knows that it is very difficult to watch a loved one die.

We have a strange tradition in our family that no matter how attached at the hip we are with the dying person, it seems that person prefers to die alone. Ironic!

My mom spent her entire adult life beside my father. They were inseparable and they loved each other very much.

My father developed dementia and Louise did everything possible to keep him at home until his last three days of life when we had no choice but to call an ambulance and have him transferred to the General Hospital in downtown Edmonton.

They admitted him into their palliative care ward and we stayed by his side every minute – only going home for a few hours each night to sleep.

Mom vowed she would remain at his side right the end as she was a dutiful wife and genuinely loved him. He adored Louise and lived his life just to be by her side. I have never seen a love like that anywhere.

Well sure enough, three days after he was admitted to the hospital he died and the saddest part was that Louise just left his room to go home to shower and eat. I drove her home and just as we pulled up into her driveway, the hospital called to say the Dad had just passed away.

Louise broke down into tears and repeated, "No! No! I should never have left his side." I reassured her and tried quickly to soothe her broken heart. I muttered something like, "Dad would not pass with you sitting by his bedside. He was too attached to you, Mom. He would hang in there forever waiting for that moment when you would leave the room."

She knew I was right, and we all came to peace with his passing. I remember all of us returning to the General Hospital after having just left it. It was a clear and beautiful July Saturday morning. As we walked up to the hospital, a stunning ray of light emerged from behind one little cloud and showered its light in a stream of rays upon us.

Truly, I have to say that at the moment, I knew that heaven was real. It is a place and Dad had just arrived.

Mom slowly got over her disappointment that she wasn't there at the moment of his death but I'm pretty sure she knew the Dad would not want her to see him die.

So fast forward to Mom's passing. Here I was alone again in her room. She had been experiencing heavy breathing for several hours now. This type of breathing is very loud and hollow sounding. In fact, when patients are dying this way, the nurses close the doors to their rooms because it is so loud you would be able to hear it throughout the entire ward.

Mom's door was closed. Her breathing was heavy. She would open her eyes occasionally, and I would say, "Hi, Mom. It's Sharon," and then kiss her face, which was not allowed but at this point I thought catching Covid was the least of her problems.

This method of dying reminded me of what women go through in labor. They are sweating, breathing heavily, and sometimes moving in and out of delirium.

The nurse came in and said to me that she was probably unaware that I was in the room. She seemed utterly exhausted. It seemed to me that this method of passing was a lot of work for the patient but natural and necessary. She seemed to be laboring into her passing, which was an interesting thought.

I was thinking that dying was truly a passing into a new life. She was being transformed from the physical existence into a spiritual one and that required a process, which no one understands.

It was necessary but inexplainable. It seemed wholesome and natural. Life was taking its course.

Mom was progressing through this passing phase over a course of about eight hours. It was now midnight. I was exhausted beyond all words. Mom was oblivious to my presence, and the nurse told me she was unaware of her surroundings.

When my father passed away, the nurse invited us into his room to see his body. I went along with the ride but deeply regretted it. Seeing my father's cold stiff body was not an image I had ever wanted implanted on my brain.

My mother was even more tender to me in my psyche and I did not want to see her body dead. I pressed my cheek against her cheek and kissed her goodbye.

I headed home and in keeping with our family tradition, she passed away shortly after I had left her room.

My memory of my mother's warm cheek remains in my psyche and I thank God every day that I did not see her die.

A person never truly knows if the decisions they make in moments like those are the right ones but I can tell you that about two years after her death, a revelation came to me that she did not want me in the room when she passed. That moment of revelation gave me tremendous peace.

Her story does not end here. The next morning, I returned to the palliative care ward to pack up her room. A helpful nurse's aide assisted me load up a cart with Louise's things. She escorted me out the back corridor to the parking lot. I had realized that the corridor is the one they use to wheel bodies out of the building and into the hearses.

I was pushing the cart and the nurses' aide was in front of the cart. As she was opening the door to the outside, she scrapped her wrist against the door and a piece of metal had caught it and cut it quite badly. She began to bleed profusely. I encouraged her to go and get bandaged up that I would be okay from here on in. She left to attend to her wound.

An amazing experience overwhelmed me at that moment. I could feel my Mom's presence all around me. Her peace, her tranquility, her joy, even her sense of humor. Such joy! Such happiness! The sense of peace was as though her entire being was resting in the arms of an angel. Her happiness was so great that her being could not hold it all – it was spilling out all around me and filling the entire tunnel. I felt it in every cell of my body.

St. Faustina wrote:

"Today I was in heaven, in spirit, and I saw its inconceivable beauties and the happiness that awaits us after death. I saw how great is happiness in God, which spreads to all creatures, making them happy; and then all the glory and praise which springs from this happiness returns to its source; and they enter into the depths of God, contemplating the inner life of God, the Father, the Son, and the Holy Spirit, whom they will never comprehend or fathom." (Paragraph 1592)

There was something incomprehensible about the joy that surrounded me in that moment. It was more than either I or my mother could contain. It was greater than ourselves and tremendously satisfying.

I loaded up my car with all the items and open the driver's door to get in to drive away. I started the car and the instant the car started the radio came on and the very first note of Frank Sinatra's voice "Cheek to Cheek" started to play on the radio station:

> Heaven, I'm in heaven
> my heart beats so that I can hardly speak
> And I seem to find the happiness I seek

When we're out together dancing cheek to cheek

Heaven, heaven, I'm in heaven
And the cares that hung around me through the week
Seem to vanish like a gambler's lucky streak
When we're out together dancing cheek to cheek.

Song by Ella Fitzgerald and Louis Armstrong

At that instant, it had occurred to me that I understood what wonder my mother could be experiencing – I believe she was being immersed into heaven itself.

Well, that's the end of my journey here on earth with my mother. I will see her again provided I make my reservation in heaven and stick to my faith because I believe that it holds the truth.

If we should ever be in a position again whereby our leaders are thinking that locking up our dying seniors is a good idea, I hope someone will remind them that we tried that once and found that with a little moral imagination, we can do better.

God bless.

To all the seniors who died isolated and alone in Canada and around the world in 2020, may you find eternal peace in heaven and know that God's angels stepped in on your journey to heaven:

"When the poor man died, he was carried away by angels to the bosom of Abraham (Luke. 16:22)

and THAT'S Canadian.

Prayers for the Sick and Dying

Job 19:25-27

But as for me, I know that my Redeemer lives, and he will stand upon the earth at last. And after my body has decayed, yet in my body I will see God! I will see him for myself. Yes, I will see him with my own eyes. I am overwhelmed at the thought!

Psalm 23

The Lord is my shepherd, I lack nothing. He makes me lie down in green pastures, he leads me beside quiet waters, he refreshes my soul. He guides me along the right paths for his name's sake. Even though I walk through the darkest valley, I will fear no evil; for you are with me; your rod and your staff, they comfort me. You prepare a table before me in the presence of my enemies. You anoint my head with oil; my cup overflows. Surely your goodness and love will follow me all the days of my life, and I will dwell in the house of the Lord forever.

Psalm 56:10-13

I praise God for what he has promised; yes, I praise the Lord for what he has promised. I trust in God, so why should I be afraid? What can mere mortals do to me? I will fulfill my vows to you, O

God, and will offer a sacrifice of thanks for your help. For you have rescued me from death; you have kept my feet from slipping. So now I can walk in your presence, O God, in your life-giving light.

Isaiah 43: 1-3

But now, this is what the Lord says—he who created you, Jacob, he who formed you, Israel: Do not fear, for I have redeemed you; I have summoned you by name; you are mine. When you pass through the waters, I will be with you; and when you pass through the rivers, they will not sweep over you. When you walk through the fire, you will not be burned; the flames will not set you ablaze. For I am the Lord your God, the Holy One of Israel, your Savior."

1 Corinthians 15:50-57

What I am saying, dear brothers and sisters, is that our physical bodies cannot inherit the Kingdom of God. These dying bodies cannot inherit what will last forever. But let me reveal to you a wonderful secret. We will not all die, but we will all be transformed! It will happen in a moment, in the blink of an eye, when the last trumpet is blown. For when the trumpet sounds, those who have died will be raised to live forever. And we who are living will also be transformed. For our dying bodies must be transformed into bodies that will never die; our mortal bodies must be transformed into immortal bodies. Then, when our dying bodies have been transformed into bodies that will never die, this

Scripture will be fulfilled: "Death is swallowed up in victory. O death, where is your victory? O death, where is your sting?" For sin is the sting that results in death, and the law gives sin its power. But thank God! He gives us victory over sin and death through our Lord Jesus Christ.

John 11:25-26

Jesus told her, "I am the resurrection and the life. Anyone who believes in me will live, even after dying. Everyone who lives in me and believes in me will never ever die.

Philippians 1:21-23

For to me, living means living for Christ, and dying is even better. But if I live, I can do more fruitful work for Christ. So I really don't know which is better. I'm torn between two desires: I long to go and be with Christ, which would be far better for me.

The Divine Mercy Chaplet

Recite each prayer on a Rosary Bead

The Our Father:

Our Father, Who Art in Heaven, hallowed by The Name: Thy kingdom come; Thy will be done on earth as it is in heaven. Give us this day our daily bread; and forgive us our trespasses as we forgive those who trespass against us; and lead us not into temptation, but deliver us from evil. Amen.

The Hail Mary:

Hail Mary, full of grace, the Lord is with thee! Blessed art thou amongst women and blessed is the fruit of thy womb Jesus. Holy Mary, Mother of God, pray for us sinners, now and at the hour of our death. Amen.

The Apostles Creed:

I believe in God, the Father almighty, Creator of heaven and earth.

I believe in Jesus Christ, His only Son, our Lord. He was conceived by the power of the Holy Spirit, and born of the

Virgin Mary. He suffered under Pontius Pilate, was crucified, died, and was buried. He descended to the dead. On the third day, He rose again. He ascended into heaven, and is seated at the right hand of the Father. He will come again to judge the living and the dead.

I believe in the Holy Spirit, the holy Catholic Church, the communion of saints, the forgiveness of sins, the resurrection of the body and the life everlasting. Amen.

On the "Our Father" bead (before each decade)

Eternal Father, I offer You the Body and Blood, Soul and Divinity of Your dearly beloved Son, Our Lord Jesus Christ, in atonement for our sins and those of the whole world.

On the "Hail Mary" beads (the ten beads of each decade)

For the sake of His sorrowful Passion, have mercy on us and on the whole world.

Concluding Doxology (after five decades)

Holy God, Holy Mighty One, Holy Immortal One, have mercy on us and on the whole world. (three times).

www.ingramcontent.com/pod-product-compliance
Lightning Source LLC
LaVergne TN
LVHW012245070526
838201LV00090B/126